a life less ordinary

a life less ordinary

a life less ordinary
interiors and inspiration

Zoe Ellison and Alex Legendre
of i gigi general store

Photography by Richard Boll

CICO BOOKS
LONDON NEW YORK

contents

Published in 2013 by CICO Books
An imprint of
Ryland Peters & Small Ltd
519 Broadway, 5th floor, New York NY 10012
20-21 Jockey's Fields, London WC1R 4BW

www.rylandpeters.com

10 9 8 7 6 5 4 3 2 1

A CIP catalog record for this book is available from
the Library of Congress and the British Library.

ISBN 978 1 908862 79 2

Printed in China

Contributing editor: Helen Ridge
Designer: Louise Leffler
Photographer: Richard Boll

RPS CICO BOOKS

For digital editions, visit
www.cicobooks.com/apps.php7

our journey

This story is about the journey of two women, Alex and Zoe, who, although from very different backgrounds, found a connection through the beauty of everyday objects, design, and antiques.

We love the romantic idea of commonplace things—from the clothes and fabrics we use in our store to the treasures, either found or given, that we surround ourselves with at home and the objects that remind us of places and people in our lives—being passed from hand to hand, leaving a piece of themselves with each person along the way.

We love the joy of finding something that makes us smile, such as a delicate piece of lace that's been untouched since the day it was packaged by hand in brown paper and tied tightly with hemp string, or of simply being seduced by the years that have passed as we hold a very old pair of tiny shoes and wonder about the child that once wore them. We are inspired by antiques that have been handcrafted by someone we never knew but who has given so much of their care, attention, and time to them. We love to be humbled in beautiful places where the sea or the sky or the trees touch our souls.

In this book we wish to share some of our stories, our thoughts, and our creativity with you and hope that you enjoy the journey as much as we have.

Love Alex & Zoe xxx

From Zoe:

A very special friendship, inspiring parents, and having the freedom to be me are the reasons Igigi came into being. I was brought up in Totnes, Devon, a well-known "alternative" town. My parents had decided to move to south-west England so my sister Lowri and I could have a progressive education. They wanted me to be encouraged to do the things that I loved, to have confidence in my own abilities, to be my own person, and to carve out my own future. Luckily for me, they succeeded.

In 1997, still in my early twenties, we made the move to Brighton, on the south coast of England. This move enabled my mother, Hazel, and I to open our own women's boutique. I needed to create something of my own, something that touched my heart and gave me a sense of purpose when I woke each morning. Using all the skills my mother had invested in me, Igigi was born. Listening to customers and making a connection felt good and honest, and helping them feel confident in their clothes was a real high. I was so busy that it was a real godsend when Alex walked through the door three months after we opened, initially as a customer but in search of a part-time job.

So, why Igigi? My mum and I came across the word in an obscure book—the Igigi were apparently the gods of the skies and of the earth in Mesopotamian mythology. But, really, what made us choose it was because we loved its sound and its shape—simple, graceful, and memorable.

The most important part of this journey was meeting Alex. She has been the most incredible inspiration and friend. She has given unconditionally every day and brought the most amazing energy and ideas to Igigi. She has been a huge part of the making of Igigi and what it is today. I look forward to the next part of our journey, dear friend.

This tiny illustrated Bible is one of Alex's most treasured possessions. Only one inch tall and bound in paper, it was given to her by an old, dear friend and is a constant reminder of their friendship.

Family and friends: where would we be without

all of you in our lives? — Alex and Zoe

From Alex:

My story couldn't be more different than Zoe's and I think that's what makes us a remarkable team.

I was born in Brighton in the early seventies, a place where my mother had settled after years of traveling. I owe my complete passion for antiques to my dad, Jamie. It was him who inspired my interested in anything old and who taught me from a very young age all about antiques. He was a "knocker boy," traveling around the country and buying from door to door, then selling it all back in Brighton (the town was a mecca for antiques, including jewelry, back then). He shared his knowledge and passion for the business with me, and I learned so much from him. I spent my childhood cleaning treasures and jewels and hearing his stories, and by the time I was thirteen, I was working the flea markets and selling my wares in the Brighton Laines.

I loathed school, finding the education system stifling. And so I spent years traveling, living in Asia and Australia, never intending to return to Brighton. I had established an exciting career for myself in Sydney as the maître d' of one of the best restaurants in the city. I loved the life and the people, and couldn't imagine living anywhere else. The turning point came when I found out I was going to have my daughter—a completely unplanned surprise. Having left home at a young age, I was always preoccupied with only caring for myself. Eventually my partner and I decided to return to England. I still wonder what would have happened if I had stayed in Sydney but fate led the way and I followed the path right to the door of the newly opened Igigi women's boutique when my daughter was three years old.

The last fifteen years have been a remarkable journey of self-discovery. Meeting Zoe and her mother was a massive turning point. From them I have learned how to believe in myself and feel confident that I really can do anything. My life has been changed forever. Zoe and I are now partners in Igigi General Store, where my passion for antiques comes into play, and I cherish every day that I spend there. I hope to pass on what I've learned to my teenage daughter who is searching for her own identity in this world.

The road trip to Igigi hasn't been a smooth one—nothing in life is ever straightforward—but I know more than anyone that you have to work hard to reap true rewards.

Opposite: Mixing cultural references and styles in a display adds intrigue. Used as wall decoration in Alex's bedroom, a gothic-style French rosary with carved wooden beads is draped over an Indian carved capitol. Similar capitols are sold in the store—the carvings all vary, with some painted, others bleached by the sun.

Below: A real sense of the past is experienced with these highly polished boots once worn by a First World War army officer. The original lasts are still inside to help the boots keep their shape. Their rich color and smooth, shiny texture have made the boots a longstanding prop in the store.

reason

The reason for Igigi is simple... we live our lives this way. We get to go to a place that we love every day. We enjoy spending our time there, whether it's working in the store with customers, helping them to find that special gift, designing a kitchen that's functional as well as original, or sourcing the furniture to make their space truly unique. We are so lucky that this is our job. One day, we focus on cooking and food shopping; the next, we get up at 5 o'clock in the morning to start a new project. No two days are the same, and no matter how crazy it gets, we still love what we do. Neither of us could imagine life without Igigi, and that includes all the marvelous people that work with us, from the café girls to the restoration team who help make every day so rewarding and stimulating.

reason

The reason for luigi is simple... we live our lives this way. We get to go to a place that we love every day. We enjoy spending our time there, whether it's working in the store with customers, helping them to find that special gift, designing a kitchen that's functional as well as original, or sourcing the furniture to make their space truly unique. We are so lucky that this is our job. One day, we focus on cooking and food shopping; the next, we get up at 5 o'clock in the morning to start a new project. No two days are the same, and no matter how crazy it gets, we still love what we do. Neither of us could imagine life without luigi, and that includes all the marvelous people that work with us, from the cake girls to the restoration team who help make every day so rewarding and stimulating.

the things that make us tickle ...

The past, memories, nature, and texture all inspire us. A seedpod captured in time, leather-bound books cracking at the spine, well-worn satin shoes—all these objects have a beauty of their own and enrich our lives.

Antique fabrics, which we source from all over Europe, form a major part of our business. Customers can buy lengths of linen or hemp from us, or we can upholster furniture for them. Each piece is quite unique and of a different width. Historically, each village would make its own distinctive cloth from hemp or cotton, using a different weave and color strip. Textured and robust, they are perfect for covering antique furniture. We have a small local restoration team that is expert at working with these vintage fabrics, which can be a hundred years old or more. The team also restores furniture, but they make sure that the integrity of each piece is preserved as they carefully strip it back and repair it.

The roll of dirty cream-colored, hand-woven linen shown here is one of the many pieces that we buy from a Hungarian father-and-son team. They visit us once every six weeks with a vanload of antique linen and hemp sacks, as well as the odd piece of small furniture which they know we will like. They have been coming to us for three years now and we count them as friends. This roll will be used for covering an armchair.

Clever combinations of unexpected materials are to be found throughout the store and in Alex's and Zoe's homes. These large hemp combs are displayed alongside wooden chopping boards in Alex's kitchen. They were originally used to comb the hemp fibers before they were spun and turned into fabric, usually grain sacks and mattress covers.

Simple shapes, like this wooden horse's head and the armchair, are easy
on the eye and appeal to our aesthetic sense. The head originally formed
part of a huge, decorative wall in an Indian house, which had been broken
up into smaller pieces for scrap. It is at least a hundred years old.

Like the horse, the Victorian armchair is sculptural in its appeal. When
we bought it, we didn't like it very much—it was too dark and masculine—
but we knew that when it had been reupholstered in dirty cream antique
hemp, it would take on a whole new persona. The hemp is incredibly
robust, perfect for a chair that sees a lot of use. The cushion is made
from a different weave of hemp, to give a mix of textures and colors.

Old, weathered, textured, and a little bit broken, this motley collection of objects in washed-out and earthy shades has a lot in common. Every piece is of special significance, whether the plaster of Paris sculpture, made by Zoe's mother and left outdoors for five years to fade and become pitted, or the bowl of camel bones, bleached by the relentless sun, which Zoe collected in the Indian desert.

We love to reclaim old things and put them in a modern space. Such pieces offer a story and a history, and bring a sense of individuality to a room that would otherwise appear bland and without character.

Whatever you choose to reclaim is all down to what draws your eye. For some deep-rooted reason, we are both drawn to faucets and taps, not the shiny chrome ones that grace modern sinks but the brass ones that show the passing of time and use with their tarnished and corroded coats and spots of verdigris.

Whenever either of us sees an antique tap, we buy it to add to our ever-expanding collection. Many of them could be installed straight away, while others would need to be repaired. Many of our finds come from Marrakesh—we love the Moroccan metalwork, and also the beaten copper of the sinks and the decorative brass wall plates to which the taps are fixed.

Recycling is a way of life for us, not just because it's the right thing to do but because it's a way of making our homes and Igigi original and unique. We have nothing that is mass-produced. Ironically, though, we recycle a lot from bygone industries. The plaster molds overleaf are from the 1840s and were used to make silverware. Nature, too, is a powerful source of inspiration. Zoe has hung a pair of antlers on the wall by her bed and uses them as a hat stand.

A gift for you, dear friend

This English tap, made of heavy brass, was probably used outdoors
originally, attached to a hosepipe by a metal nut. It always makes
us beam with delight—we love its shape, and it is beautifully made.
The verdigris and tarnish only add to its appeal.

simple shapes create unusual shadows

Casts that last

friendship

The meaning of friendship is, for us, summed up beautifully in these words attributed to Roy Croft. It begins: I love you / Not only for what you are

But for what I am / When I am with you.

I love you / Not only for what

You have made of yourself,

But for what / You are making of me.

During the course of our friendship, we have both changed enormously because of the other person. We have learned so much from each other, and continue to do so, and both of our lives have been enriched as a result. It is a mutual exchange of love and respect.

Our friendship is key to the success of Igigi. We have more or less identical tastes, which drew us to each other in the first place. During the course of the working day, we share confidences. We make business decisions jointly, and we are always honest with each other because we value the other's opinion. Feeling safe and secure with each other means that we have been able to take Igigi in different directions and continue to do so. But to keep the friendship and business healthy, we lead separate lives outside of work.

friendship

The meaning of friendship is, for us, summed up beautifully in these words attributed to Roy Croft. It begins: I love you / Not only for what you are

But for what I am / When I am with you.

I love you / Not only for what

You have made of yourself,

But for what / You are making of me.

During the course of our friendship, we have both changed enormously because of the other person. We have learned so much from each other, and continue to do so, and both of our lives have been enriched as a result. It is a mutual exchange of love and respect.

Our friendship is key to the success of Igigi. We have more or less identical tastes, which drew us to each other in the first place. During the course of the working day, we share confidences. We make business decisions jointly, and we are always honest with each other because we value the other's opinion. Feeling safe and secure with each other means that we have been able to take Igigi in different directions and continue to do so. But to keep the friendship and business healthy, we lead separate lives outside of work.

Sometimes the hardest things to do are the most important. Loving someone fully, respecting them and forgiving them for all their faults, is perhaps the most difficult. Letting another know how much you care for and value them is actually the beginning of an amazing journey of self-discovery.

The simplest gifts can express these sentiments so powerfully. Zoe inscribed different messages on these paper tabs and gave them to Alex for one of her birthdays. Each tab starts with "I love" and gives a reason why.

These love letters have inspired maple veneer tabs that are sold in the store, with sixty-five different inscribed messages, from "I love the way you smell" to "I love the way you dance when you're alone." There are also blank ones for writing your own messages.

The idea of expressing how you feel has been taken an unlikely step further. A message is laser-cut into a dried white butter bean, which is then sown. Incredibly, the message appears on the first leaf when it pushes through the soil.

There are no two ways about it—our friendship is a very special one. You can't spend this much time with someone and not feel this way.

Our connection, which started fourteen years ago at the igigi women's boutique, has grown and developed until we've reached a point where we can almost read each other's minds. We recognize and acknowledge the strengths and weaknesses in ourselves and in each other, and neither of us feels we have to fight to be in control.

We respect each other's choices and decisions. Listening to the other's ideas and being objective is crucial, although sometimes listening doesn't always mean hearing! That's something we've learned along the way.

Then there is trust. Neither of us wants the ethos of the shop to be anything other than how it is now, and if we trust each other to always keep that honesty, surely we hold the key to our own success!

Our vision for how we want the store to be for the next season is something we both see clearly. We lead each other through our ideas and the outcome is this unique place. Bringing our different attributes to the table is probably how the Igigi General Store was born.

We really appreciate what we have and how well we work together. It's taken a lot of hard work to get here and the road hasn't always been smooth. Igigi is like our baby that's all grown up and it's now really showing us that all the hard work was worth it—including the sleepless nights!

One of our favorite things to do together is go on shopping trips. We set off in our battered blue van for the day and return with the back of it bursting and a lot closer to the ground! The journey always takes much longer than it should. On the way, we discover things along the roadside, such as seed heads, which we know will look gorgeous in the store, and start to load the van with them. These discoveries en route, together with the animated conversation, often inspire the next season's theme for our store and interiors.

On these trips we are easily sidetracked and each one soon turns into an excuse to buy for ourselves and for each other as well. We egg each other on, and "Why don't you just buy it?" becomes a frequent refrain, although it's not used indiscriminately. Knowing each other so well means that we can tell whether the object in question is more than just a whim.

We are always on the lookout for new sources and suppliers, but we do have our favorite shopping destinations. It's actually quite rare to find a store that's completely in tune with your aesthetic, so once you find one, never let it go. This stone foot in Alex's home was discovered at one of our favorite haunts in London's Portobello Road. It's around 400 years old and probably Iranian. Alongside are glass domes on stone bases protecting delicate pieces of coral. Tucked in between is a dried hydrangea bloom, one of our favorite flowers—whether dried or in full bloom, their beauty is constant.

"Sometimes fate is like a small sandstorm that keeps changing direction. You change direction but the sandstorm chases you." These words are from Haruki Murakami's novel "Kafka on the Shore." Zoe had the complete passage lasered onto a piece of maple veneer and gave it to Alex as a birthday card.

These words are hugely important to us, as they speak about fate and destiny, and how we all are our own destiny, responsible for creating everything around us. Igigi was born as the result of Zoe following a path that she had set for herself but changing direction whenever that felt the right thing to do. Along the way, Alex joined her on that path.

All the images shown on the facing page are tokens of friendship that we have given to each other during the course of our journey together. Nothing is new or mass-produced, but neither is anything outrageously expensive. The pheasant plume collar, from the Eaton Nott store in Brighton, is pure drama and makes a remarkable wall decoration.

The photograph above encapsulates the fun and the love we share at Igigi. It shows the two of us celebrating with Alby, who manages the Igigi women's boutique for Zoe's mother. A few years ago, on a scorching September day, we hosted an outdoor fashion show on the lawns of Brunswick Square, which is just around the corner from the store. We had the catwalk and the pumping music, and our staff and customers were the models, including one wonderful lady who was in her seventies. It was all done very professionally and was a huge success, with the money generated going to a local children's charity.

The event started out as an aside in a conversation but then, as so often happens with us, the creative juices started to flow—we got the spark of an idea and that's where it took us. We run our store in exactly the same way.

The ivory-colored, silk-embroidered shawl that Alex wore to the event, shown in close-up on the left, is an amazing piece of craftsmanship from the early 1900s. Something so gorgeous shouldn't be allowed to languish unseen, cocooned in tissue paper in a drawer. It deserves to be worn and its beauty shared. If something is too fragile to be worn or used, then simply display it.

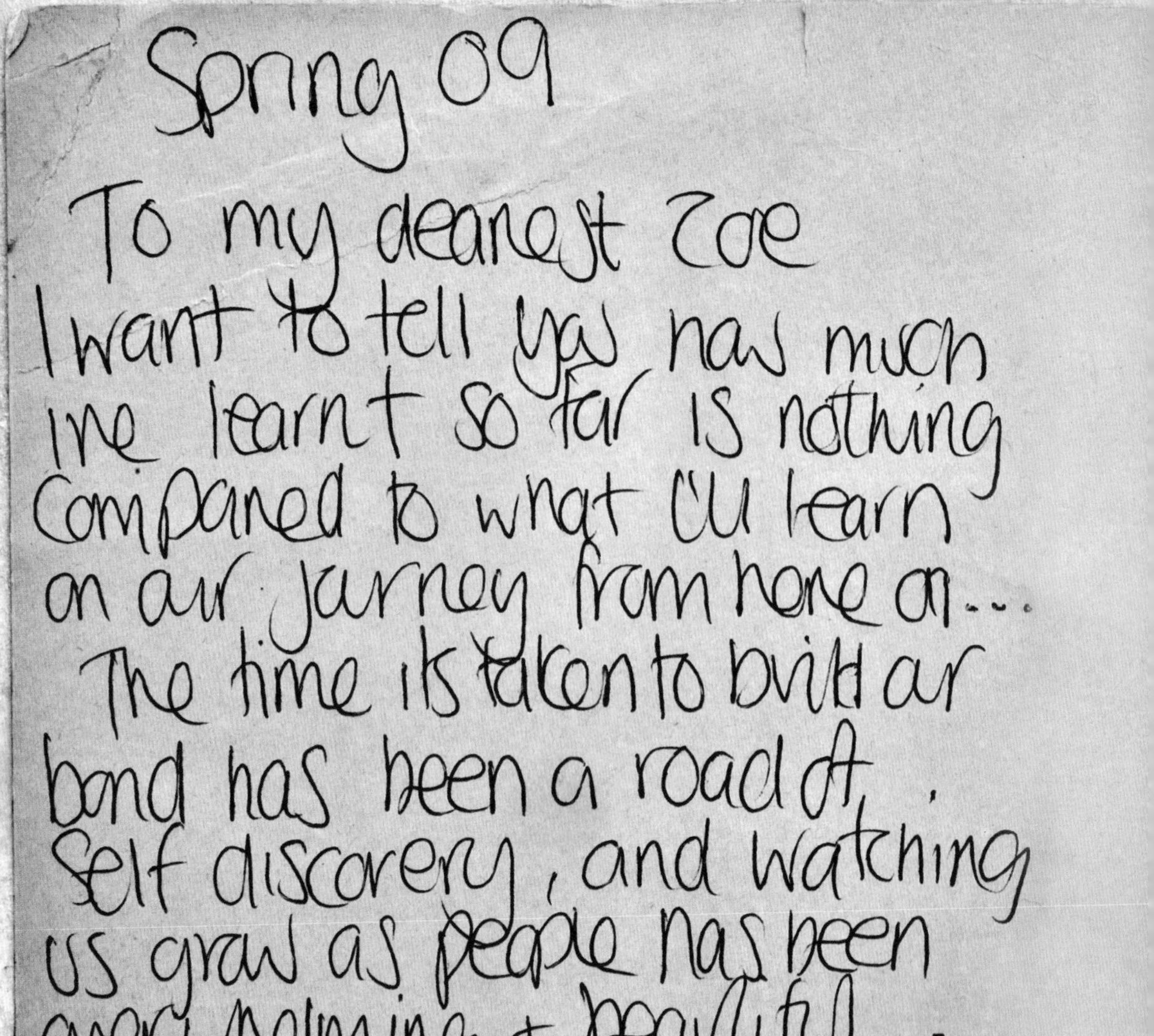

Spring 09

To my dearest Zoe
I want to tell you how much
Ive learnt so far is nothing
compared to what I'll learn
on our journey from here on...
The time its taken to build our
bond has been a road of
self discovery, and watching
us grow as people has been
overwhelming + beautiful...
Heres to our future! Alex xx

In The Spring Time

Sharing cherished possessions is one sure way to express friendship and love. This well-thumbed and beautifully illustrated book of Spring is from a series about the seasons from the 1930s, which Alex has owned and treasured for almost all her life. She inscribed it on the inside cover and gave it to Zoe as a gift, to celebrate the growth of their business and their friendship.

A gift for you, dear friend

shop

Every part of Igigi has been created with love and attention to detail, all of it such a far cry from the rundown greengrocers shop that it was when we bought it. A laser-etched slab of slate says when we are open, while a French reclaimed door with metal fretting welcomes you inside. The original Dutch gable roof is the only one on the street. The design of the store reflects our genuine love for what we do and what we share with other people. It's this, we believe, that sets Igigi apart from other stores. Obviously sales are important or we wouldn't have a business, but how we make it work really does matter to us. Igigi is like a house, with all the customers our guests. At their suggestion, we created the upstairs café, which seats around fifteen. It's a simple affair in an amazing space, with a menu of delicious homemade dishes such as soups, salads, and cakes.

shop

Every part of Igigi has been created with love and attention to detail, all of it such a far cry from the rundown greengrocers shop that it was when we bought it. A laser-etched slab of slate says when we are open, while a French reclaimed door with metal fretting welcomes you inside. The original Dutch gable roof is the only one on the street. The design of the store reflects our genuine love for what we do and what we share with other people. It's this, we believe, that sets Igigi apart from other stores. Obviously sales are important or we wouldn't have a business, but how we make it work really does matter to us. Igigi is like a house, with all the customers our guests. At their suggestion, we created the upstairs café, which seats around fifteen. It's a simple affair in an amazing space, with a menu of delicious homemade dishes such as soups, salads, and cakes.

We change the look of Igigi with the seasons, although it always retains its muted, earthy color palette. Here it is shown in its autumn livery, where the trademark palette has become warmer and darker, in preparation for winter. Giant antique clamshells and scented candles adorn the trestle table with its natural-colored linen runner. A grain shovel stands alongside the reupholstered vintage sofa. The space is decorated like a home but with every single piece, from the sofa to the chandelier, for sale.

A few of our favorite things on sale at one time or another in the store: balls of hemp string piled high in bowls; a traditional Hungarian abacus with wooden counters; vintage linen napkins tied with string; old rusty nails; an antique Indian shrine. Nothing is mainstream or mass-produced, and everything has a history all of its own.

Opposite: The almond-shaped
crystal beads from an
unusual pewter chandelier
from France. Originally
designed for candles,
it has flat wax cups, but
now it's wired and can be
seen hanging in the store
on page 51.

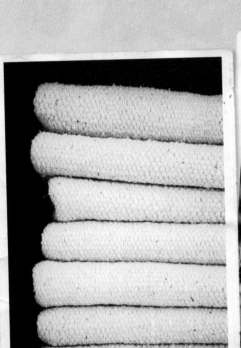

This page: More delights
from Igigi, including the
Sustain Ceramics bowls
and plates, made by
Sarah Jerath with her
own homemade clay. Left
unglazed on the outside,
their unfussy shapes, each
one slightly different,
are wonderfully tactile.
The strands of bells, made
to look antique, jingle
pleasingly when hanging
on a door. Antique linen
cushions are soft and full
of character.

As well as running Igigi General Store, we also offer a design service, which ranges from advising on upholstery and soft furnishings to designing entire houses.

When it comes to interior design, the most important thing for us is to create a space that is practical and can be lived in, as well as looking beautiful and feeling relaxed. The first question asked when we start a consultation is, "How do you live?" Knowing how clients live on a day-to-day basis is key to the designs we create for them. No design is ever the same because our clients are all individuals with different needs.

Function is always the most important part of any space. If it doesn't do what you or your family wants it to, then it won't ever feel truly comfortable. It will also never be fully used, and what's the point of that? Many of us spend our lives paying for our home, and the reward is that we should be able to live and breathe every part of it.

Through the store we show how even a full space can be made to feel uncluttered and and calm. Every part of it is filled with creativity, and great care is taken over the way we display all our finds.

The shelves are our canvas,

and the furniture our backdrop.

The basic principles of display can be seen at work at the back of the store on pages 58-9. Large sliding doors, which lead to the tiniest of courtyards, make the space light and airy, and every item is given space to breathe so it can be fully appreciated.

Using our trademark color palette, with its muted, earthy tones, means that we can display the most unlikely objects together. Floating shelves accommodate vintage linen cushions and traditional Indian wooden oil holders, while petrified logs of wood have become pedestals for shallow bowls of handmade paper tags. Propped against the opposite wall are old hemp combs beneath Shaker pegs displaying embroidered silk jackets and straw hats. On the reclaimed French farmhouse table, scented candles look much more appealing piled high underneath vintage glass domes. A cloth-covered tailor's dummy makes an unfussy prop for displaying a vintage mother-of-pearl necklace and African clay beads.

We deliberately design every incarnation of the store to resemble a home, so that customers will have more of an idea how various pieces might look in their home before buying. Whenever we go shopping for stock, we always have particular customers in mind. They don't know it but the next time they're in the store and fall in love with something, it's quite likely that we would have bought it especially for them.

Stripping it bare—renovating the shop.

capturing the past

Our main aim at Igigi is to introduce unique and vintage products to our customers. We often rework old pieces to give them a new purpose in life and create heirlooms for the future with sustainable or antique fabrics and designs. Each one of these is lovingly restored or handcrafted, with beauty and longevity in mind, by local craftsmen and women who share our sense of honesty, ethics, and pride.

Some vintage pieces, though, simply do not stand the test of time. The seat cushion of a leather armchair may be beyond restoration but instead of patching it with new leather, we would preserve its sense of history by reupholstering it in antique linen.

capturing the past

Our main aim at Jojoi is to introduce unique and vintage products to our customers. We often rework old pieces to give them a new purpose in life and create heirlooms for the future with sustainable or antique fabrics and designs. Each one of these is lovingly restored or handcrafted, with beauty and longevity in mind, by local craftsmen and women who share our sense of honesty, ethics, and pride.

Some vintage pieces, though, simply do not stand the test of time. The seat cushion of a leather armchair may be beyond restoration but instead of patching it with new leather, we would preserve its sense of history by reupholstering it in antique linen.

These antique tools, with their nicked and worn wooden handles, are still used to restore and reupholster old pieces of furniture, such as the leather chair with its arm worn away through at least a century of constant use. The leather apron, made by our upholsterer six years ago, still has a long life ahead of it. Some objects are not meant to be restored. The leather boots will never be worn again and deserve to be left as they are, conjuring up images of the person who once owned them and the roads they traveled. Likewise, the antique mirrors propped up against the wall. The foxing of the glass makes them even more beautiful and evokes a powerful sense of history.

Those who knew Igigi in its previous incarnation, as a fruit and vegetable store, would not recognize it today—we took the space back to its bare bones. We painted the walls in a type of creamy colored plaster, which is one of our specialties, to make a soothing backdrop, and added reclaimed wooden floorboards. These are wide to create a sense of space. As you walk through the front door, you feel as if you are going back to a bygone age, when life was calmer and shopping was something you could do at your leisure.

The serving counter (see pages 68-9), which was last seen in a French bar, now looks as if it has always belonged here. It had been painted a horrible brown color and we spent three solid days removing the paint with stripper, which left it looking quite raw. All it then needed was a light polish. Irish woolen cardigans for the fall season hang from a French dresser top behind the counter. Generally, clothes are sold in the separate women's boutique, but sometimes they add just the right finishing touch to a display. Inside the glass cabinet, rolls of hemp string, used for wrapping, stitching, and knitting, are decorative as well as practical. Lengths of raffia for tying up parcels hang from a nail and make a gorgeous, tactile wall decoration, while sheets of handmade banana paper from India are sold as wrapping paper. Above the counter, Original BTC handmade ceramic lights, inspired by traditional designs, look good whatever the time of day.

The walls of the basement are covered in the same creamy colored plaster as the floor above, but water leaking from the road had caused one wall to become very marked and stained. After eventually fixing the water problem, we decided to leave the wall as it was—the stains left behind simply add character and individuality to the space, as you can see overleaf.

Sometimes the best thing to do is leave alone.

Texture and soft earthy neutrals unite all the elements of these displays, from the armchair reupholstered in antique linen and the delicate lace of a child's christening gown to the tailor's dummy with its torn and tattered fabric. The simplest things, often recycled or found, can make the most effective decoration. The patterns made by a dried sunflower head and the paper-thin petals of garlic flowers invite you to peer closely to fully appreciate their intricate beauty. Smooth and shiny pieces of white porcelain and a ball of hemp string, meanwhile, invite your touch.

When the store is closed, we often stay behind and play around with ideas for Igigi's next look. This tabletop scene is the result of one such session, which we created for a new winter season, using a mix of old and new. The theme revolved around texture and the heritage of the British Isles. A vintage Remington typewriter, still very much in working order, joins a vintage Harris tweed jacket, new Irish woolen cardigans, and a wooden hat last. "New Season's Stock" was typed on the paper in the typewriter, and customers and their children added their insightful and often humorous comments, which we kept. The versatile pouffes underneath the simple rustic table are covered in antique Hungarian linen, to be used as either coffee tables or seating. The same approach to display, mixing the practical with the purely decorative, works equally well at home.

The uneven glass of vintage jars, their lids mislaid long ago,
adds a quirky, distorted charm to whatever is stored inside.
Here, the jars create a unified display for the practical and
the purely decorative, including a collection of buttons and
a pair of baby shoes originally worn by Zoe's mum.

home

Home is a tiny word for such an important place. For all of us, it's where we want to feel safe and warm, protected and comfortable. It's also a place from where you draw strength and where you feel your most authentic self. As might be expected, there is a certain similarity between our two apartments, which are like a pared-down version of Igigi. The muted, earthy palette of the store has its origins in our homes. Wide, reclaimed wooden floorboards and our trademark plaster-effect walls feature in our homes, too. We also display our treasures in the same way, grouping them by color, texture, or shape—whichever is most pleasing to the eye.

home

Home is a tiny word for such an important place. For all of us, it's where we want to feel safe and warm, protected and comfortable. It's also a place from where you draw strength and where you feel your most authentic self. As might be expected, there is a certain similarity between our two apartments, which are like a pared-down version of Jojo. The muted, earthy palette of the store has its origins in our homes. Wide, reclaimed wooden floorboards and our trademark plaster-effect walls feature in our homes, too. We also display our treasures in the same way, grouping them by color, texture, or shape—whichever is most pleasing to the eye.

Zoe's home

Taking a bath is one of my favorite pastimes, so there were no shortcuts taken with the decoration of one of the most important rooms in my home. Soft gray-tinted plaster walls make the most soothing backdrop, while the floorboards are smooth and warm underfoot. The freestanding cast-iron tub is so deep that the water comes up to my chin. It's also big enough to share with my sister's children, Louis and Marly, but that's not quite so relaxing! Even though the room is small, I didn't want it to be a purely functional space. The rusty radiator isn't plumbed in. It's pure decoration, like the dried sunflower head on top, with its exquisite coloring—a conker-brown around the outside with a dark mushroom center. The plastered-over traditional Turkish oil jar serves as a table base, with a reclaimed slab of wood on top.

Filled with tangible memories and connections, the living room is very much
a reflection of me. The filled-in fireplace is the perfect home for the Indian
papier-mâché refrigerator, inlaid with mirror, which I picked up on my
travels. Making a seamless join with the walls, the cream-colored plaster
hearth leads the eye up to the painting by my father.

Antique cupboards are often not deep and practical enough for use today, but removing the door from a basic modern cupboard and replacing it with a decorative old one solves the problem. Thin linen curtains, bleached by the sun to a white-cream, provide all the privacy required, while the unobstructed natural light highlights the delicate chandelier that I made myself from seashells.

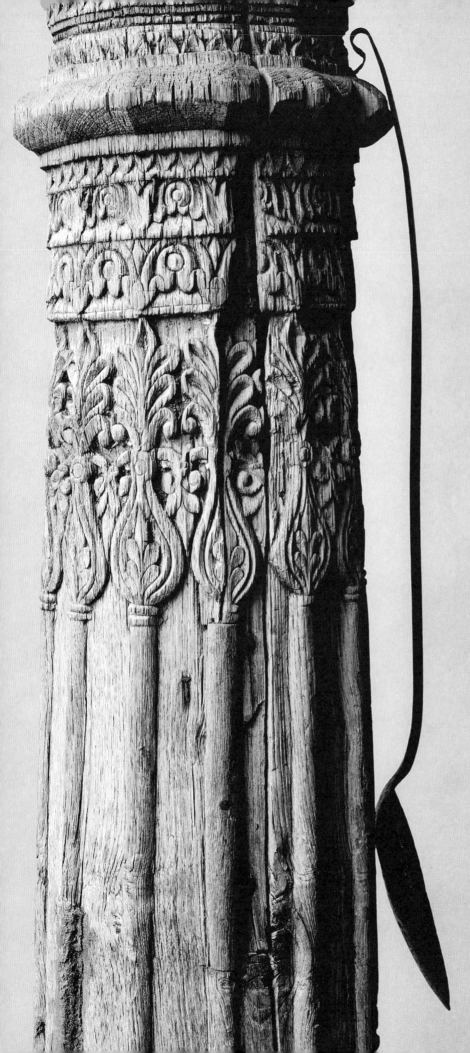

My home is a sanctuary, very
simple and stripped back, and
there's nothing hidden behind
the scenes. In spite of its small
size, the apartment never looks
cluttered, even though it's
full of treasures that I have
collected over the years. One
wall of the narrow hallway is
crammed with an ever-changing
collection of photographs of
family and friends, all in dark
mahogany-colored frames that I've
collected to give unity (see
pages 136-7). Having the display
on just the one wall and painting
the walls the same color as the
woodwork opens the space out.
A tiny, old "school" radiator,
stripped back to the iron and
then lacquered, throws out an
enormous amount of heat while
fitting the space and looking
good all at the same time.

The compact, open-plan kitchen,
with its gray-blue cabinets,
makes effective use of a tiny
corner. Carved and weathered
Indian pillars have a practical
as well as decorative role.
An oversized cast-iron serving
spoon hanging from one of them
is an original decorative touch.
Above the hob, a painted eggshell
splashback is discreet as well
as practical because it can be
wiped clean.

JUMBO OATS
BARLEY FLAKES
TOASTED WHEAT
ROLLED OATS
RYE FLAKES
STRAWBERRY
PINEAPPLE
APPLE
MULBERRIES
PISTACHIOS
CURRENTS
COCONUTS

EAT
EAT

The kitchen leads to the conservatory, where, with the back doors open, I like to have breakfast. This is one of my favorite times of the day, shared with my partner Andy, and often with my niece and nephew, who emerge from my sister's home downstairs, half-dressed and sleepy-eyed.

Always remember life is short.

Forgive quickly, kiss slowly!

Laugh in love uncontrollably

And never regret anything that

Made you smile.....

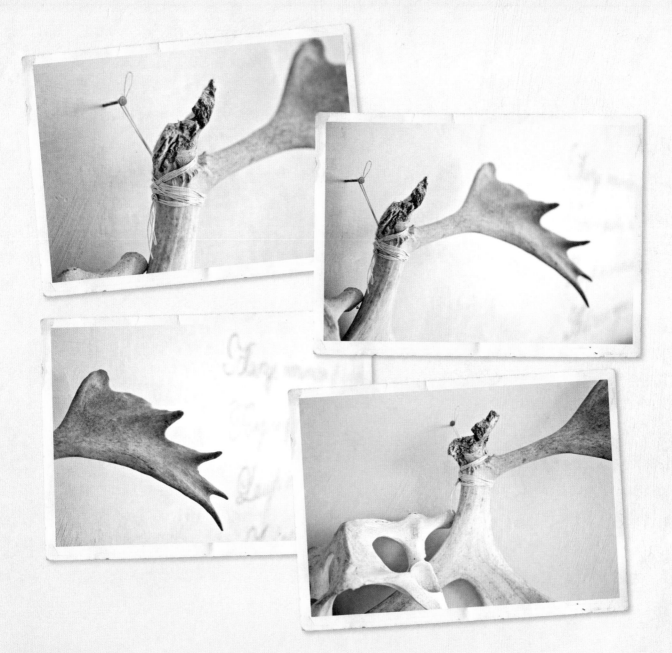

My bedroom is a wonderfully calm and comfortable space. These words, painted over the bed, were texted to me one year on Christmas Day by a dear friend. I've never been able to confirm who wrote them originally but they moved me so much that I re-created them on the wall in an ocher pigment mixed with water. They are a gentle reminder every day of how to live my life. The stags' horns, tied to a nail with an intricate knot, take the place of a conventional wall display.

Overhead lighting is often unflattering and, although beautiful, this antique chandelier is no exception and isn't even wired up. It is purely for decoration. Instead, soft atmospheric lighting is provided by low-voltage lights, fitted flush to the floor. Sandblasted back to the pure oak, the vintage French bed, reupholstered in antique linen, is romantic in the extreme.

Always remember life is short.
Forgive quickly, kiss slowly.
Laugh in love uncontrollably
And never regret anything that

The unrestored vintage mirror, with its distressed edge, gives a studied reflection of the gilt and glass chandelier and the painted quotation. In the bricked-up fireplace underneath, an old trunk with leather straps provides attractive storage for blankets.

Victorian pine is pale with a lovely chalkiness about it, as can be seen in these antique wardrobes. On top, the vintage leather bags and a pheasant plume collar—a gift from Alex—are for decoration only, as are the 1920s silk coat and dress hanging from one of the doors, their colors complementing the wood to perfection.

Alex's home

My home isn't just about me—it's also about my daughter, my husband, and the dog.
That said, it does bear my mark with all the things that I've collected over the years.
Even though the colors are pale and muted, this is a very lived-in and comfortable space.

The chesterfield sofa is a solid piece of furniture that cost next to nothing to buy from a house clearance sale. Reupholstered in antique linen, it will last for a good many years yet. The rusty and scratched military chest, over one hundred years old, makes very interesting storage with a palpable sense of history. All the walls were stripped back to the lath and plaster, then decorated with our raw cream-colored plaster. Together with the stripped-back and scrubbed original floorboards, they make a soothing neutral backdrop for all the furniture in their muted earthy tones.

Underneath the Victorian pine desk, which makes a characterful alternative to the run-of-the-mill sink surrounds, are vintage cheese boxes used to store much of the bathroom paraphernalia. Towels are hung from a Shaker-style peg rail, while toothbrushes are stored in an Indian oil carrier. Fresh and dried flowers in ceramic pitchers, and pukca shells, mementoes of different places I've lived in and loved, decorate the room.

In unifying tones of creams, grays, and browns, the bedroom is a soothing retreat from the outside world. To keep it that way, I am always on the lookout for interesting storage, such as the bashed leather cases on top of the wardrobe, used for storing photographs and other precious memories, and the dowry trunk by the side of the bed. The distressed mirror (opposite), with most of its gilding missing, was created out of an antique French frame to which I added new glass.

Like all the other rooms, the bedroom is filled with vintage treasures (see pages 102-3). A dowry trunk covered in hide provides much-needed and unusual storage—I am an unashamed hoarder—while the vintage child's dress hanging from the wardrobe is just for decoration. Above the chesterfield sofa (shown below) is the only painting in the apartment—I generally prefer to hang interesting objects for decoration. It's a provocative original by Zoe's father, and I adore it. The sofa belonged to my Grandma in Ireland, so I have a real emotional attachment to it. I had it reupholstered in antique French linen. The linen bed pillows were put there by chance one day, but they worked so well that they've stayed. Vintage ivory beads are draped over an Italian mercury glass mirror (opposite), made all the more interesting by the widespread foxing.

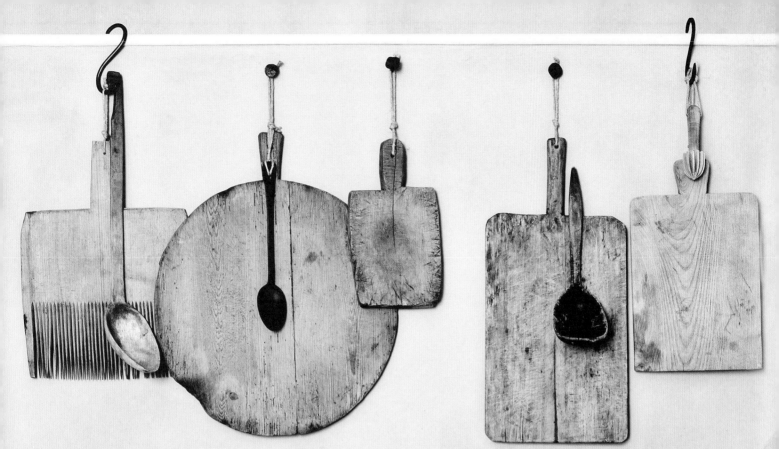

The kitchen is where the family gathers to eat and to talk, and to show love by cooking, preparing, and sharing.

J.L. DURAND
37 ST AUBIN   C.

ROLAND DURAND   K8
ST AUBIN LE DEPUNT 37

Just a few of the many treasures of a compulsive gatherer:
a vintage-style railway clock; wooden Dutch clogs; textured
ceramics; distressed mirrors; dried flowers; vintage baskets...
With so many disparate items, grouping the displays and
keeping their tones consistent make the overall look soothing
and calm. Nothing appears out of place, not even Dobby, our
very old and very fat Jack Russell.

Practical items used every day can also form part of a cohesive display. Jars, pitchers, and bowls in similar tones all look at ease on the kitchen dresser (see page 106). On an adjacent wall, a selection of antique breadboards and cooking spoons line up with a hemp comb above a stripped-back church pew, their textures and tones working wonderfully well together. An antique sack has been made into the seat cushion. Beneath is the "wine cellar," created out of French apple crates. A salt-glaze ceramic bottle (see opposite), traditionally used for ale, is the centerpiece of this harmonious display with a well-worn and textured breadboard and a pile of random bowls, some about 400 years old. The miniature succulent is an endearing contrast in scale and color. Antique breadboards also double up as serving platters (see left).

There are times when you just can't restore a piece of furniture as you would like. The seat cushion of this wonderful leather chair was beyond repair—finding the exact match of leather would have been impossible. Instead, I decided to keep the integrity of the chair by replacing the seat cover with antique linen. The matching cushion ties the whole thing together.

inspiration

Living in a city makes it particularly important to us to introduce nature into our homes. Fresh flowers are always welcome but not essential. We regularly forage in the woods and on the beach, returning home with pockets and bags bulging with branches, dried flower heads, pebbles, and seaweed. Nearby Shoreham Beach is a haven of dried flora, especially in September, when various plants roll along the beach like tumbleweed. Our inspiration also comes from our travels, and both of us have brought many, many treasures back with us as mementoes of happy times. How you display all these things is crucial. Insignificant pieces will be overlooked if left on their own, but grouped with other objects they become powerful. Changing your collections from time to time is invigorating, allowing you to appreciate other treasures.

inspiration

Living in a city makes it particularly important to us to introduce nature into our homes. Fresh flowers are always welcome but not essential. We regularly forage in the woods and on the beach, returning home with pockets and bags bulging with branches, dried flower heads, pebbles, and seaweed. Nearby Shoreham Beach is a haven of dried flora, especially in September, when various plants roll along the beach like tumbleweed. Our inspiration also comes from our travels, and both of us have brought many, many treasures back with us as mementos of happy times. How you display all these things is crucial. Insignificant pieces will be overlooked if left on their own, but grouped with other objects they become powerful. Changing your collections from time to time is invigorating, allowing you to appreciate other treasures.

Display your inspiration

Storage can, and should, be decorative. Zoe's favorite necklaces are draped over a Victorian tailor's dummy in her bedroom. Not only are they always on show and close to hand, the dummy is a gorgeous thing in its own right. Beautifully weathered, its journey can be seen through the tears, nicks, and holes in its fabric.

The enormous wooden bowl on Zoe's bedroom floor is probably more than a century old, with the noticeable crack in it adding to the appeal. It also has a practical role, storing a collection of horn, wood, and bone bracelets, which deserve to be seen.

Nature provides the color palette and the inspiration for these displays. Intricate clusters of coral, dried seaweed bleached by the sun, and a pile of stones covered in white lichen, all collected by Zoe, evoke memories of times and experiences, both near and far away. Nestled in among them, giving extra depth to the display, is a motley collection of manmade treasures, including a brass Indian deity about an inch tall, ceramic bowls, and a pair of vintage children's boots.

The displays in our homes show off our favorite things,
which means that we can enjoy them every day and also
share that enjoyment with others. Trusting your instincts
when choosing what to have on show is essential. Start
looking at things in a different way and experiment, grouping
the unexpected together, and recognize beauty in imperfection.

These beautiful necklaces of ivory, seeds, coral, and bone are far too beautiful to be locked away in a drawer or jewelry box. The back of a wooden chair provides a neutral backdrop, to highlight their charms.

Texture and a natural palette of muted earthy colors give a depth to simple shapes and make it easy to show off cherished possessions. Recycling and looking at things differently opens up a whole world of creative display. Take rust, for example. A sheet of rusty metal becomes a striking piece of art or a lovely textured background for a display of white plates; old and bent rusty nails make decorative and unusual hooks for hanging jewelry. "Home," created out of flaking, rusty letters in warm browns, is a fitting welcome on the wall in Alex's hallway.

Collecting objects that others in the past have loved, whether or not you ever knew their owners, and making those things special in your life is good for the soul. Flaking paintwork, the cracks of time in leather, the foxing of mirror glass, give such pieces all the more character.

If, on your travels, you fall in love with something but can't think how it would fit into your home, buy it all the same. Don't miss an opportunity and regret it all your life—we know from experience that the perfect other pieces will present themselves sooner or later.

If you love something, display it and share it with others, but don't restrict yourself to walls and shelves. Take advantage of doorknobs; use a pile of books to act as a pedestal; dress a tailor's dummy. Long necklaces of ivory, seeds, coral, and bone, draped over the back of a wooden chair (see pages 122-3), are shown off to the full, with their rough and smooth textures and contrasting shapes crying out to be touched. A vintage, rich brown leather jacket hanging from an industrial-size door hinge makes an intriguing outdoor display with the contrasting textures of rope and grainy wood and the mix of harmonious grays and browns (see pages 124-5).

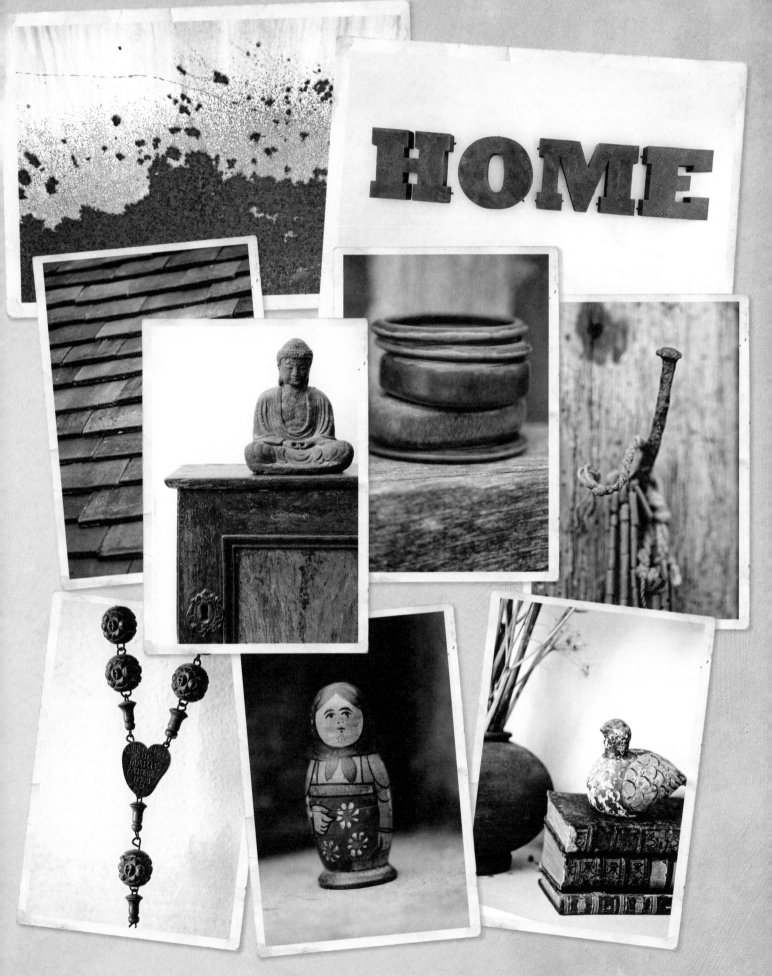

heirloom

Heirloom is a very evocative word, interpreted differently by each and every one of us—after all, one man's rubbish is another man's treasure. We feel that it's our responsibility to take care of old things—they are a tangible connection to the past and allow us to connect with their original owners.

Personal possessions, such as jewelry, photographs, and clothes, that are handed down through families have particular resonance. Whether or not they are used as originally intended, become a decorative object in their own right, or are given a completely different role, is entirely up to us. Heirlooms involving children are particularly moving. The vintage boots opposite tug at the heartstrings. Although worn and with deeply creased leather, these neatly hand-stitched boots have lasted as a pair for about one hundred years. Items that have fared less well over time can perhaps be recycled. Rescue what you can from tattered clothes and make them into something else. Recycle the fabric from an old chair and use the sections that aren't threadbare to make cushions.

heirloom

Heirloom is a very evocative word, interpreted differently by each and every one of us—after all, one man's rubbish is another man's treasure. We feel that it's our responsibility to take care of old things—they are a tangible connection to the past and allow us to connect with their original owners.

Personal possessions, such as jewelry, photographs, and clothes, that are handed down through families have particular resonance. Whether or not they are used as originally intended, become a decorative object in their own right, or are given a completely different role, is entirely up to us. Heirlooms involving children are particularly moving. The vintage boots opposite tug at the heartstrings. Although worn and with deeply creased leather, these neatly hand-stitched boots have lasted as a pair for about one hundred years. Items that have fared less well over time can perhaps be recycled. Rescue what you can from tattered clothes and make them into something else. Recycle the fabric from an old chair and use the sections that aren't threadbare to make cushions.

Zoe's teddy bear was her
grandmother's, with a well-
documented history, which makes
it all the more fascinating.
Bought from a traveling salesman,
he was given to her on her fourth
birthday and never left her side.
She would whisper all her secrets
to him and tell him stories.
Inherited by Zoe in 2007, when
her grandmother died, he is as
precious to her now, sitting in
her bedroom with the secrets and
stories still safe and sound.

Photographs of generations long
gone convey an overwhelming sense
of history, particularly if they
are of your family. The sepia
print on page 129 is of Zoe's
grandmother, holding her precious
teddy bear, and her brother;
the picture here is also of her
grandmother. Continuing this
sense of connection, photographs
of today's generation will become
the heirlooms of the future.

Correspondence between family
members of previous generations
allows a peep into lives that
are so different from ours. An
envelope written in a cursive
script with a dip pen that blots
the ink speaks volumes. Unlike
photographs, there will be
very few such letters for our
ancestors to learn from in
the future.

We all show our personalities through the collections we acquire during the course of our lives. These could be from our travels, heirlooms from parents, gifts from children, or simply those things that have caught our eye in antique stores. Both the vintage child's dress and the letter, with the postmark betraying its age, are vital connections with the past.

B. Higgs
Barcilley Road
St Brite
Wallington

This old printer's type case is used to display tiny treasures that might otherwise get lost. Things get added but rarely is anything removed. After all, if you love something enough, you wouldn't want to replace it.

Every inch of space along one wall in Zoe's hallway is devoted to photos of family and friends. The frames are a mix of shapes, sizes, and styles but what they all have in common is their color, and if they weren't black to start with, Zoe painted them.

MIZ

A collection of cushions and pillows—both vintage linen prints and embroidered—in soft textures and tones, introduce sophistication and comfort to a teenager's bedroom. The antique linen with the botanical motif (left) once covered an old chair but was becoming increasingly threadbare. Not wishing to lose the fabric completely, pieces of it were salvaged and reinvented as a cushion cover.

Too fragile to be worn, this vintage embroidered silk jacket with a tasseled fringe still deserves to be admired. The oversized costume jewelry brooch, remarkably intact for its age, brings a touch of glitter to the ensemble.

vintage

For us, vintage clothing means romance, nostalgia, and glamour. It is a very particular look, often decorative, with beading or lace, although it can also be very plain but with something that sets it apart, such as intricate stitching, a monogram, or cloth or mother-of-pearl buttons. This sepia print of Zoe's mother sums up all we love about vintage. With her hair pinned up, she looks utterly demure in a black velvet shawl with gold embroidery. It is a piece that she has kept, not to wear but for the memories it brings back and because it is beautiful. The detail on page 145 shows a black-beaded vintage dress bought by Alex but which she never intended to wear. She has no idea who it belonged to originally but she fell in love with it. It hangs on the bedroom wall, a wonderfully tactile alternative to a conventional wall display.

vintage

For us, vintage clothing means romance, nostalgia, and glamour. It is a very particular look, often decorative, with beading or lace, although it can also be very plain but with something that sets it apart, such as intricate stitching, a monogram, or cloth or mother-of-pearl buttons. This sepia print of Zoe's mother shows us all we love about vintage. With her hair pinned up, she looks utterly demure in a black velvet shawl with gold embroidery. It is a piece that she has kept, not to wear but for the memories it brings back and because it is beautiful. The detail on page 145 shows a black-beaded vintage dress bought by Alex but which she never intended to wear. She has no idea who it belonged to originally but she fell in love with it. It hangs on the bedroom wall, a wonderfully tactile alternative to a conventional wall display.

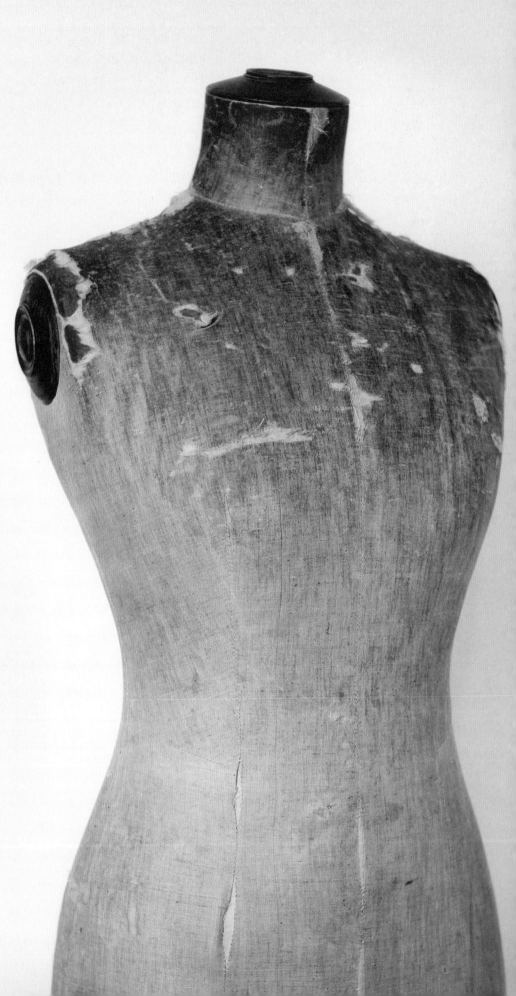

This whalebone corset with metal stocking buckles was a present from Alex to Zoe and is displayed to perfection on a tailor's dummy. Interesting and decorative in its own right, it makes a very versatile prop. As well as having the corset relaced, Alex included a fitting as part of the gift—never do anything by halves! This work of art, which dates back to around 1910, epitomizes a time when ladies were expected to be nothing but feminine, even if that meant struggling to breathe and having little room for maneuver!

Pretty shoes that have danced at extravagant balls have a romantic story to tell. The delicate silk pair on page 150 are well worn, meaning that they were probably well loved, too. More rustic and homespun but equally romantic is the summer hat made from rush grass, displayed with woven basketweave beads, alongside a linen dress and jacket, all in subtle earthy tones. Hanging from simple hooks, they make a subtle and evocative display.

A backdrop of roughly hewn timbers is the perfect backdrop for a rustic but romantic outfit in contrasting textured fabrics. White-painted floorboards show off the pretty silk shoes perfectly (left).

This little girl's
dress is the natural
dusty sand color of
raw silk. It is hand-
stitched and decorated
with delicate silk
embroidery, with lace
around the neck. It
must have been washed
many, many times
because it is so worn
and soft. Although
it's a dress meant
to be worn every day,
the love, care, and
attention to detail
that went into its
creation are all too
apparent. So that
nothing will detract
from its charm, it
is displayed in the
simplest possible
way, hanging from an
invisible pinboard
painted the same color
as the wall.

A favorite era for us is the 1920s, a time of optimism and abundance, when everything was felt to be possible. We've made all sorts of clothes inspired by that time, including wide-legged pants (trousers) with side zippers. They provoked so many compliments from customers when we wore them in the store, we had them made up to sell.

In the same way that we love muted earthy tones for decorating our homes, we prefer to wear those colors, too. Occasionally, we are able to dress in vintage clothes, such as this beautiful creamy colored embroidered silk cape, which is not so fragile as you might think. The detailing is incredible, from the embroidery to the lace and bobble trim. Where it came from, we have no idea, but that makes it all the more intriguing. It might even have been a religious garment worn by a man!

The child's undergarment shown overleaf is made of silk with mother-of-pearl buttons. As flimsy as a shadow, the unbelievably delicate fine weave can be appreciated in the detail photograph. The beauty of this piece lies in its honest simplicity.

Sunlight filtering down highlights the tulle of a vintage wedding dress (see pages 158-9). What could be more romantic?

The detailing on this hand-stitched child's undergarment, from the mother-of-pearl buttons to the embroidered edging, is breathtaking. It deserves nothing more obtrusive than pins to fix it to the wall.

setting the scene

There are absolutely no rules to follow when putting your home together. Be adventurous and shun convention, and be inspired by your surroundings. Above all, be true to yourself and fall in love with what you create. Creating a space for a special celebration is probably the most fun you can have with interior design. Then you can really let your imagination run riot, inventing a temporary world that might otherwise remain in your dreams. Any space can be transformed by the objects it contains and the way in which they are displayed. In the vast 400-year-old barn, shown in all its rustic glory on pages 164—5, we have created a stunning but intimate dining area that is like a stage set, where the lighting is the star of the show.

setting the scene

There are absolutely no rules to follow when putting your home together. Be adventurous and shun convention, and be inspired by your surroundings. Above all, be true to yourself and fall in love with what you create. Creating a space for a special celebration is probably the most fun you can have with interior design. Then you can really let your imagination run riot, inventing a temporary world that might otherwise remain in your dreams. Any space can be transformed by the objects it contains and the way in which they are displayed. In the vast 400-year-old barn, shown in all its rustic glory on pages 164–5, we have created a stunning but intimate dining area that is like a stage set, where the lighting is the star of the show.

Hanging over the dining table and suspended from the rafters with rope is a cluster of three small chandeliers, linked together to form one extravagant piece of decoration. The contrast created between the coarseness of the rope and the sophistication of the chandelier is particularly appealing. The chandeliers aren't actually wired up but their role isn't to illuminate the table. They are pure decoration—a sculpture and an ornament rolled into one.

This creation would work equally well for an outdoor gathering, where you could hang the chandeliers from a tree. If you don't have any chandeliers, simplify the idea and hang jam jars with tea lights inside. The effect will be just as magical.

Steering clear of convention invariably produces the most atmospheric results. Look to nature for inspiration. Create drama by dressing a table with the unexpected, such as driftwood or stags' horns, and intertwine them with tea lights. Instead of elegant glass vases filled with ephemeral florist flowers, have chunky stone urns filled with long-lasting potted plants. Foraging in nature never fails to turn up the most amazing finds. Draped with lights, a fallen tree could replace a conventional Christmas tree. Dried flower heads in a chipped porcelain pitcher make a lovely table centerpiece.

It is the people in our lives that make them worth living, so it's important to show them how much we care for them. Cooking and sharing food is one of the most basic and rewarding ways to do this, and the combination of good food and beautiful presentation is key. Making everything look and feel good is what we do—whether it's for interiors, clothes, or food—and we cut no corners in achieving it. Even if the food is incredibly simple, the way in which it is served speaks volumes.

Adapting objects plays a major part in the way we serve food and make the whole event a visual feast. Thinking beyond the realms of an object's original function is really exciting. Use the big stone platters traditionally used for rolling chapatis as cheeseboards, or wooden chopping boards for serving afternoon tea. Both of us have a thing about wooden spoons, and inevitably we have made collections of them. Full of character, one day they are stacked in the corner of the kitchen cabinet, the next they're used as part of a table setting.

In the barn, we have covered a long makeshift table with a soft blue linen cloth that cascades dramatically to the earth floor, and topped it with a textured linen runner. Sophisticated, matching dining chairs give an instant clear message that this is a special occasion, a celebration, an event. Easily achievable, the look is elegant but inviting, designed to make every guest feel welcome.

No table setting is identical. All the glasses are hand-blown with an organic feel about them, while the handmade Wonki Ware ceramic plates and bowls from South Africa are also totally unique. These things we adore for their individuality. The silverware is a mix of copies of French vintage hotel silverware and traditional, bone-handled Sheffield cutlery. The matte, brushed silver-plate of the copies contrast beautifully with the slightly tarnished metal of the traditional.

An antique armchair reupholstered in linen forms part of an intimate vignette, breaking up the expanse of one wall. Hungarian milking stools, which have been left outdoors to weather beautifully, are used as a side table and a pedestal for a lamp. With a shade made in Sussex from antique linen, and the base a recycled Turkish urn, the lamp is an unconventional but successful mix of component parts. A tailor's dummy, meanwhile, makes an unexpected but delightful prop. The neck of the mannequin against the lacework of the vintage dress is simply gorgeous.

Seen during the day, a shaft of sunlight pinpoints the table as it shines through a tiny, high-up window, but as the guests start to arrive and the darkness settles, the rest of the barn will disappear into the shadows, creating the most romantic space, where the flickering flames of the tea lights are reflected in the drops of the chandeliers.

Fresh, seasonal salads, made from leaves, herbs, nuts, and fruits, lightly tossed in simple dressings so as not to overwhelm the flavors, make the most delicious and nutritious dishes. Slow-roast belly of pork is another favorite of both of ours. Amazingly easy to make—it's the time in the oven that makes all the difference—we use the recipe (see overleaf) at many of our parties, both at home and at the store.

Alex's roasted belly of pork

Slow-roasted belly pork on the bone with glass-shattering crackling and a sticky sweet sauce of pears and shallots is one of my favorite dishes when I'm feeding lots of friends. It works especially well if you don't have the time to stand over a hot stove but really want to impress a large group with a delicious treat!

good pork belly on the bone, enough for
  dinner and leftovers
enough shallots for 3-4 per person
garlic—I'm in love with the whole clove bulb!
  Use around 6 big cloves for six people
pears (hard ones, such as conference, are
  ideal), at least one per person
2 cans of ginger beer—a hot one! And you can
  always drink what you don't use
a few fresh bay leaves
good sea salt flakes—I like to use smoked
  Maldon salt flakes when roasting meats
freshly ground black pepper

Preheat the oven to its highest setting while you prepare the dish. It has to be really hot when the meat goes in or you risk soggy crackling! Take the pork out of the fridge while you prepare the veg and pears.

Choose an ovenproof dish just large enough to fit the pork snugly. Place the peeled shallots and whole, unpeeled garlic cloves in the dish.

Quarter the pears and slice out the centers to get rid of the little core and any pips. Add the pears to the dish, skin side down, so the entire base of the dish is covered. Now pour over enough ginger beer to almost cover the fruit and crush the fresh bay leaves in your hands to gently break their skin (this releases the flavor).

And that is the base for your pork—easy!

Rinse the pork in cold water and dry using good-quality paper towels or a clean dish towel. Score the skin with a very sharp knife—don't cut too deeply and try to keep the score marks only a fraction of an inch apart. It's all in the preparation and I promise it's going to be worth it.

Place the pork on the nest of bay, shallots, pears, and garlic and rub in the sea salt flakes, getting them right into the skin. Sprinkle with a little black pepper and pop into the middle of the oven, keeping it on high for 25 minutes.

After 25 minutes, turn the oven temperature down to a low-medium heat. I say low-medium heat because everybody's oven temperature is different, so if you know your oven go with your gut instinct, if not stick with 180°C/350°F/gas mark 4. Don't forget to turn the temperature down or you'll have a disaster on your hands!

Now you can put your feet up for around
3 hours, depending on the size of pork joint.

When the cooking time is up, remove the pork
from the oven and let it rest for 30 minutes.
Lay a piece of foil over the top of the dish,
but don't tuck it in. While it's resting, you
should be able to compile your salad or veg.

You'll need a large, flattish serving dish
and a sharp knife. Gently lift the pork onto
the platter and place the pears, garlic, and
shallots around the pork. They should still
be whole but very soft and fragile, so spoon
them with care.

Glide the crackling off the top of the pork
with a long, sharp knife and broil or grill
on a wire tray to really crisp it. Leave
behind the fatty bit under the skin (this can
be removed and thrown away). Cut down the
bones to separate into ribs and then replace
the crackling on the top. Job done!

All the juices should have separated in the
warm oven dish, so spoon off all the oil and
just reheat the beautiful stock, then strain
and serve.

Autumn salad

This goes so well with the pork belly and
again it doesn't take very long to do. Of
course, you can add your own twist, like
pomegranate or any other seasonal yumminess.

Rip figs, washed and chopped roughly with
  the skin
Melon, peeled and chopped
Green peppers, sliced
Chicory
Romaine lettuce
Green basil
Chopped chives
Watercress

Combine all the ingredients together in a
large bowl. Dress with good olive oil and
simply season to taste.

Quick potato salad

Baby new potatoes, boiled until tender
Roasted garlic
Red onions, finely chopped
Chopped chives
Salt and pepper

Add any creamy dressing such as mayo or crème
fraîche with a spoon of Dijon mustard.

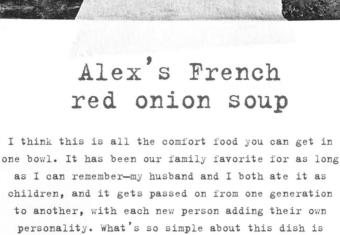

Alex's French red onion soup

I think this is all the comfort food you can get in one bowl. It has been our family favorite for as long as I can remember—my husband and I both ate it as children, and it gets passed on from one generation to another, with each new person adding their own personality. What's so simple about this dish is the ingredients—you don't really need anything you wouldn't already have in your kitchen store.

The soup has become a regular on the menu at the café, served just the way I like it with my dad's recipe for welsh rarebit used for the cheesy croutons—a delicious combination with the rich dark soup.

6-8 large red onions, finely sliced
a pinch of fresh thyme
7 tablespoons (100g) organic salted butter
a splash of mild olive oil
half a teaspoon of sugar
2 tablespoons flour
$3\frac{2}{3}$ cups (850ml) homemade or good-quality
bought beef stock
a generous glass of wine that you would drink
(not an old, half drunk, dusty bottle)
a nip of brandy

a baguette, some delicious Gruyère cheese, mustard
powder, and an egg yolk for the croutons

Soften the onions in a large shallow pan with the thyme, half the butter, and a splash of oil. Stir continuously to make sure the onions don't stick to the base of the pan. When they have browned and taken on a silky, rich consistency, add the sugar and season. Stir in the flour and keep it moving while it cooks for a few minutes. Now add your wine and stock, and simmer for 30 minutes.

While the soup simmers, prepare the croutons. Slice the baguette and toast one side. Finely grate some Gruyère and mix with an egg yolk and a generous pinch of mustard powder. Spread the cheese mixture on the untoasted side of the baguette slices and broil/grill until golden.

Add the brandy and remaining butter to the soup and you're ready to serve.

Home-made cherry ice cream

This is our simple summer ice cream recipe—
just the thing for making the most of plump
and juicy cherries during their all-too-short
season. You can make it in just minutes, and
this simple and not-too-naughty dessert is
great for everyone on a hot summer's day.

Feeds 6, with enough leftover for second
helpings!

¼ cup (60ml) cherry juice or cordial
½ cup (125ml) fat-free milk
1 scant cup (220ml) vanilla yogurt
1 cup (250ml) heavy (double) cream
½ cup (100g) superfine (caster) sugar
a pinch of salt
1 cup (150g) sweet cherries, pitted
2 teaspoons almond extract

Place the cherry juice, milk, yogurt,
and cream into the bowl of a blender.
Add the sugar, salt, cherries, and almond
extract. Purée until only small pieces
of the cherries remain.

Pour into a 6-cup/1.5-litre ice-cream maker
and freeze according to the manufacturer's
instructions.

We guess if we were asked to sum up Igigi, it would be as a fantasy world but it is one that we really do inhabit. It is where objects can be both practical and beautiful, where we can upcycle things not for fashion's sake but because we see their real potential as something else with a valid use in our customers' homes and our own.

Having the store isn't just a career for us, it's our lives, and that's why it's so important to be honest and enjoy every moment—we never sell something we wouldn't use ourselves, and we always advise truthfully. Of course, it's hard to be upbeat all the time but, honestly, our days are so diverse, it's very difficult to become bored or disillusioned.

The store is a haven not only for shopping but also for sharing our inspiration and creativity with customers, and for them doing the same for us. We call this "feeding the soul." Although we never break free completely from our neutrally inspired color palette, we do introduce strong naturals when the seasons dictate it, such as deep bricks and rusts in the fall, and golden ochers in the spring.

Igigi gives us the best excuse to travel, sharing our finds with grateful customers who might not have the time to venture very far themselves but who love to feel part of the journey. We trade with diverse suppliers in all corners of the world, who find our way of buying stock intriguing: we group things and hold stock back for long periods of time to create our own collections based on the color of the different woods or the types of fabric that suit the season. Then we find handmade soaps and candles to match the palette, making the store cohesive and calm.

The return Camel ride as
in imaginations chamber.
Back in through the gate.
Did I feel the freedom of
the desert one morning?
Did I take myself undeniably
with me?
I want to imagine it
differently tomorrow.
So that I am with a
whole lot of other people
on camels!

love you
xox

Traveling has played a big part in both our lives for many years. Long before Igigi, we both lived in far-flung corners of the world, meeting and breathing other cultures. We believe passionately that traveling and immersing oneself in other cultures broadens the mind and the vision. Long may it continue!

Our memories of traveling, and those of our families, remain crystal-clear, embodied in photographs, postcards, and hastily scribbled notes. Either on open display or easily accessible elsewhere, they are a constant reminder of what we have experienced and learned.

time to say goodbye

It is very important to us that everyone involved with Igigi—customers and staff alike—takes something away from it that will add value to their lives. After all, they give so much to us. Many of our customers become regulars and are almost like family, while our staff, who are encouraged to bring a part of themselves to the business, offer their insight and experience, not only to the customer but also to us. We also hope that you, the reader, will take something from this book. Perhaps it will help you to tap into your creativity and pursue your own vision. Perhaps it will inspire you to be courageous and take risks, so that you are no longer hindered by a lack of confidence.

If this book does nothing but inspire you, then for us our job is done.

Alex's words, inspired by the "Holstee Manifesto." The words
hang in the store as a constant reminder of the way in which
we want to live our lives.

Life is short, so live every day as if it's your last.
If you are not happy with your life, then change it.
If you feel like time is slipping by, slow down.
If you are searching for the love of your life, then stop.
They will come to you.
Make every day have a memory to last.
Feel every emotion, happy or sad, pain or elation.
Life is about what you learn and what you give back.
Say something positive to a stranger and feel good.
Give yourself freely and expect nothing in return.
You will be rewarded.
Share your love, your joy, and the things you have learned
on your journey. This will be somebody else's courage.
Travel the world and feel every moment of the experience.
Love with passion, give freely, take with grace.
Speak honestly, walk with pride, and learn constantly.
Once you have the tools, you can build the life you dream of.

with thanks to:

Hazel and Peter, Alby, Ging and Mizzy, Andy, Jayne,
Geraldine, Ann, Sarah Small, Lowri Pez and the kids

Hana, Caroline, Faye, Alex C, Meg, Maria Jose,
Sarah, Sadie, Ruth, Shelly, Louise, Alice, Georgia,
Betty, Emily, Emma P, Xenia, Olga

Mandy, Melody, Kathryn

Peter and Fiona, Peter, Claude, Tilly and the
girls, Denisa, Zina, Teresa, Bazza and the boys,
Stuart and his team, Badger and Denes

Gezza-bel, Ben and Barney, Pat and Martin, Kim,
Saville and Sheila, Dan and Perry, Timmy and son,
Joe, George, Susannah and Tony, Mr Mathew

Justin, Baz the Spark, Edd, Jimmy-cricket, Janet
and Miles, Frank, Sticky and Nick, The Russells,
Liz and Randy, Dickie, Dave-Windows, Christopher

Leon and Pete, Phil, Stewart Van-Tempest, and,
lastly, Richard Boll

And to all the many others that play a huge part
in Igigi: great big thanks to you for your hard
work and patience.

Love Zoe & Alex xxx

index